Meditations on Death:
Preparing for Eternity
Thomas à Kempis

GRAPEVINE INDIA

Published by

GRAPEVINE INDIA PUBLISHERS PVT LTD

www.grapevineindia.com
Delhi | Mumbai
email: grapevineindiapublishers@gmail.com

Ordering Information:
Quantity sales: Special discounts are available on quantity
purchases by corporations, associations, and others.
For details, reach out to the publisher.

First published by Grapevine India 2023
Copyright © Grapevine 2023

Welcome to our Christian book collection!

For access to more Christian audiobooks,

send a blank email to

thegoodchristian10@gmail.com.

Contents

1. ON THE DAY OF ETERNITY AND THE TROUBLES OF THIS LIFE

The Learner: How happy are those who dwell for ever in the city that is above! How bright is the day of eternity! It is a day upon which night casts no shadow, but one for ever lit by the very Truth; a day for ever happy, for ever safe, a day that never changes into the contrary. Oh, how I wish that day had already dawned, and all these things of time come to an end! For the Saints, that day is already shining, bright with a radiance that goes on and on; for us who are still making our earthly pilgrimage, it shines only from a distance; we can see its reflection, so to speak, only in a looking-glass.

2. Those who are townsmen of the heavenly city know how joyful the day is there; we, the outcast children of Eve, know how bitter and wearisome the day can be on earth. Yes, the days of time are few and evil indeed, full of sorrow and trouble. Here man is befouled by many sins, enmeshed in many passions, brushed close by many fears. He is tormented by many cares, dragged this way and that by many strange sights, entangled in many kinds of folly. Many an error surrounds him, many a hard task leaves him exhausted; he is burdened with temptations, enfeebled by pleasures, racked with want.

3. Oh, when will these evils come to an end? When shall I be freed from the wretched slavery of sin? Lord, when shall I think only of you, find in you my full measure of gladness? When shall I be really free, with nothing to hinder me, nothing to drag me down in mind or body? When will there be lasting peace, peace for ever safe and never to be disturbed, peace both within and without, peace that in every way stands unchanged? Good Jesus, when shall I stand in your sight and see you? When shall I gaze upon the glory of your kingdom? When will you be all in all to me? Oh, when shall I be in that kingdom of yours which you have made ready from all time for those you love? Here I have been left behind in enemy territory, a poor outcast in a land where every day there is fighting, every day disasters most dire.

4. Comfort me in this my exile; assuage my grief; it is to you that I sigh with all my longing. Whatever this world can offer me by way of comfort is nothing but a burden to me; I long for the bliss of your close company, but I am unable to reach so far. I yearn to hold fast to heavenly things, but I am weighed down by the things of the time, by passions far from dead. With my mind I long to rise superior to all these things, but my body compels me to be their unwilling slave. Thus it comes about that I, poor piece of humanity, am the theatre of civil war, a burden to myself, with the spirit trying to soar aloft, and the body endeavouring to stay below.

5. What I go through inwardly, when my mind is groping its way towards the things of heaven, and, during my very prayer, a crowd of worldly thoughts comes rushing into my head! Do not go far away from me, my God, do not turn away in anger from this servant of yours. Dazzle them with the stroke of your lightning, and scatter them; shoot forth your arrows, and so put to rout all the drifting thoughts sent by my enemy. Gather my senses together and fix them on yourself; make me forget all that is in the world; give me the power to hurl back and to scorn all mental pictures of evil deeds. Come to

my help, O everlasting Truth, so that no empty folly may sway my heart. O heavenly sweetness, come to me, and all that is foul will flee at sight of you. Forgive me, also, and in your mercy grant me pardon for all the times I think of anything besides you in time of prayer; because, to confess the truth, I am usually in a state of great distraction. Often enough I am not where my body is, whether standing or sitting, but wherever my thoughts carry me to. Wherever my thoughts are, there am I; and my thoughts are usually with the things I love. What comes most readily to mind is something naturally pleasant or found by experience to be agreeable.

6. It was this that made you, the very Truth, say plainly: *Where your treasure-house is, there your heart is too.* If I love heaven, I readily think of heavenly things; if I love the world, I share the world's gladness when it rejoices, and am sad when it is thwarted. If I love the body, I often picture to myself bodily delights; if I love the spirit, I love thinking about spiritual matters. Whatever it is that I like best, those are the things I love talking and hearing about; and I bring home mental pictures of them with me from the world outside. But happy is the man who for your sake, Lord, has, so to speak, given all things created notice to quit; the man who gets tough with nature and crucifies the lusts of his body with the burning desires of his spirit. Such a man has put his conscience at rest and can offer you unblemished prayer; by closing the door on earthly interests, both in his life and in his heart, he is worthy to mingle with the choirs of Angels.

2. ON LONGING FOR ETERNAL LIFE, AND THE JOYS PROMISED TO THOSE WHO FIGHT TO GAIN THAT LIFE

The Beloved: My son, when you feel the desire for everlasting bliss streaming into you from on high; when you thirst to leave that body in which you are now, as it were, camping for a time, so as to be able to gaze on my glory, that glory on which there falls no shadow of change: open your heart wide, and welcome this holy inspiration with all the longing you have. Thank me again and again for my divine bounty in dealing thus with you so generously, visiting you in my mercy, stirring you with the fire of my love, uplifting you with my strength, and so preventing you from falling down again into those worldly ways to which you gravitate so naturally. You must not take this favour to be the result of your own meditations, your own exertions; it is yours only because the grace of heaven has come down to help you, because God has looked on you in love. Its purpose is to make you advance in holiness, to make you more deeply humble, better prepared for conflicts yet to come; it is to make you cling close to me with all the love of your heart, to make you long to serve me with willing devotion.

2. There are often fires burning, my son, but not a flame shoots upward without smoke beside it. That is the way with a lot of people who are afire for heavenly things; the flame is there well enough, but they are not free from the temptation of bodily desire. Thus it is that, for all the longing they put into their prayers, they do not offer them solely for the honour of God. That is often the way with your own desire, though you may have persuaded yourself your prayers were going to be perfectly sincere; but no prayer can be called perfect or free from blemish when there is some tincture of self-interest in it.

3. Do not ask me for things to make life pleasant and comfortable for you; ask for what is acceptable to me, for whatever brings me honour. If you look on things in the way you should, you ought to prefer my way of ordering things, and keep to it, rather than ask for the fulfilment of your own desires or for the keeping of something you have desired before. I know what your desires are; I have heard what you so often sigh for. You would like to be at this moment amid the freedom and the glory of the children of God, enjoying your eternal home and the abounding happiness of the heavenly country; but the time for that has not yet come. You are still, for the moment, in another kind of time—wartime it is, a time of toil and trial. You long to be filled with the supreme good, but that bliss is not to be arrived at now. I am speaking of myself; wait for me, the Lord says, until the coming of the kingdom of God.

4. There is still a time of trial for you on earth; you must be tested in many ways. Sometimes you will be given consolation, but it will not be granted you in full abundance; so take heart and be strong, whether doing or enduring what goes against nature. You have to clothe yourself in a new kind of manhood, change into another kind of person. Often you will have to do what you dislike, and forgo doing what you would like to do. Other people's interests will prosper, your own make no headway; others will be listened to when they speak, but people will take no notice of anything

you say. Others will ask for things, and get them; when you ask, your request will be in vain.

5. People will say a lot of nice things about others; no one will say a word about you. Others will be given this or that position of trust; you will be reckoned good for nothing at all. Naturally, this kind of thing will make you sad now and then, but if you bear it all without saying a word, you have taken a great step forward. These are the ways—these and many others like them—by which a faithful servant of the Lord is usually tested, to see how he can renounce himself and break his own will in everything. There is hardly anything in which you need so much to die to yourself as to see and suffer things that are opposed to your own wishes. This is especially so when things are ordered to be done which to your mind are quite out of keeping and completely useless. Being under obedience to another, as you are, you dare not stand up to one higher in authority, and so you think it hard to have to live your life at another's beck and call and disregard your own feelings.

6. But think, my son, of the reward these hardships are going to win you; think how soon they will end, how great is the prize you will be given. Then you will not feel the weight of them; instead, they will comfort you and be a strong support to your will to endure. In return for the free surrender of what little choice you have in earthly things, in heaven you shall always have your own way. Yes, there you shall find all you have ever wanted, all you could ever desire. There every kind of delight will be yours to have, and you will never be afraid of losing it. There will your will and my will be ever as one, and you will desire nothing I do not desire, nothing for yourself alone. There shall be no one to withstand you there, no one to complain, no one to hinder or thwart you; but all you have ever desired will be there together, giving joy to your powers of love and filling them to the very brim. There, for the shame you have suffered, I will give you glory; in place of the garb of mourning, a robe of honour; instead of the lowest place, a seat in my kingdom for ever. There your obedience shall be rewarded in the sight of all; your hard penance shall be turned to joy, and your lowly subjection receive a crown of glory.

7. During this present life, then, behave humbly towards all men, and do not mind who says this or who orders that, but take great care that whenever anyone asks you for something or makes some suggestion, whether he be your superior, your equal, or one below you, take it all in good part and with unfeigned willingness try to do what they say. Let other men have their ambitions in one direction or another, one man priding himself on his ability in one field, another in something different, and getting praised for it any number of times; you must take pleasure in none of these things, but only in being slighted and in my good pleasure and honour alone. This is what you must desire: that in you, whether by your life or by your death, God may always be glorified.

3. ON THINKING ABOUT DEATH

Your time here is short, very short; take another look at the way in which you spend it. Here man is today; tomorrow, he is lost to view; and once a man is out of sight, it's not long before he passes out of mind. How dull they are, how obdurate, these hearts of ours, always occupied with the present, instead of looking ahead to what lies before us! Every action of yours, every thought, should be those of a man who expects to die before the day is out. Death would have no great terrors for you if you had a quiet conscience, would it? Then why not keep clear of sin, instead of running away from death? If you aren't fit to face death today, it's very unlikely you will be by tomorrow; besides, tomorrow is an uncertain quantity; you have no guarantee that there will be any tomorrow—for you.

2. What's the use of having a long life, if there's so little improvement to shew for it? Improvement? Unfortunately it happens, only too often, that the longer we live the more we add to our guilt. If only we could point to one day in our life here that was really well spent! Years have passed by since we turned to God; and how little can we shew, many of us, in the way of solid results! Fear death if you will, but don't forget that long life may have greater dangers for you.

Well for you, if you keep an eye on your death-bed all the time, and put yourself in the right dispositions for death as each day passes. Perhaps, before now, you've seen a man die? Remember, then, that you have got the same road to travel.

3. Each morning, imagine to yourself that you won't last till evening; and when night comes, don't make bold to promise yourself a new day. Be ready for it all the time; so live, that death cannot take you unawares.

Plenty of people die quite suddenly, without any warning; the Son of Man will appear just when we are not expecting him. And when that last hour comes, you'll find yourself taking a completely different view of the life that lies behind you. How bitterly you will regret all that carelessness, all that slackening of effort!

4. If you hope to live well and wisely, try to be, here and now, the man you would want to be on your deathbed. What will give you confidence then—the confidence which ensures a happy death? To have despised the world utterly; to have longed earnestly for advancement in holiness; to have loved discipline, to have taken penance seriously, to have obeyed readily, to have renounced self, to have put up with everything that was uncongenial to you for the love of Christ.

You see, there is so much you can undertake while you are still in health—what will you be able to manage, when illness comes? Illness doesn't often change people for the better, any more than going on pilgrimage makes Saints of them.

5. You will have friends and relations to pray for you? Don't, for that reason, leave the business of your soul to be settled later on.[19] You will be forgotten sooner than you imagine; better make provision now, by opening a credit account for yourself, than trust to the good offices of other people. You, so unconcerned about yourself

today—why should other people concern themselves about you tomorrow? No, here is the time of pardon; the day of salvation has come already. The more pity you should make so little use of it, your opportunity for winning a title to eternal life. Some time, you'll know what it is to wish you had another day, even another hour, to put your life straight; and will you get it? There's no saying.

6. My friend, my very dear friend, only think what dangers you can avoid, what anxieties you can escape, if you will be anxious *now*, sensitive *now* to the thought of death! Make it your business so to live, today, that you can meet death with a smile, not with a shudder, when it comes. If that moment is to be the beginning of a life with Christ, you must learn, now, to die to the world; if you are to find free access to Christ then, you must learn now to despise everything else. A body chastened by mortification means a soul that can face death with sure confidence.

7. Poor fool, what makes you promise yourself a long life, when there is not a day of it that goes by in security? Again and again, people who looked forward to a long life have been caught out over it, called away quite unexpectedly from this bodily existence. Nothing commoner than to be told, in the course of conversation, how such a man was stabbed, such a man was drowned; how one fell from a height and broke his neck, another never rose from table, another never finished his game of dice. Fire and sword, plague and murderous attack, it is always the same thing—death is the common end that awaits us all, and life can pass suddenly, like a shadow when the sun goes in.

8. Once you are dead, how many people will remember you, or say prayers for you? To work, friend, to work, as best you may, since there is no saying when death will come, or what will be the issue of it. Hoard up, while there is still time, the riches that will last eternally; never a thought but for your soul's welfare, never a care but for God's honour. Make yourself friends now, by reverencing God's Saints and following their example; when your tenancy of this life is up, it is they who can give you the freehold of eternity. Live in this world like some stranger from abroad, dismissing its affairs as no concern of yours; keep your heart free, and trained up towards God in heaven—you have no lasting citizenship here. Heaven must be the home you long for daily, with prayers and sighs and tears, if your soul, after death, is to find a happy passage to its Master's presence.

4. ABOUT THE JUDGEMENT, AND HOW SINNERS ARE PUNISHED

At every turn of your life, keep the end in view; remember that you will have to stand before a strict Judge, who knows everything, who cannot be won over by gifts or talked round by excuses, who will give you your deserts. What sort of defence will you make before One who knows the worst that can be said against you—poor, sinful fool, so often panic-stricken when you meet with human disapproval! Strange, that you should look forward so little to the Day of Judgement, when there will be no counsel to plead for you, because everyone will be hard put to it to maintain his own cause! Now is the time to work, while there is a harvest to be reaped, now is the time when tears and sighs and lamenting of yours will be taken into account, and listened to, and can make satisfaction for the debt you owe.

2. Nothing so important, nothing so useful, if you want to clear your soul of that debt, as to be a man who can put up with a great deal. Such a man, if he is wronged, is more distressed over the sin committed than over the wrong done him; he is always ready to say a prayer for his enemies, forgives an injury with all his heart, and is quick to ask forgiveness of others, and you will find him more easily moved to pity than to anger. And all the while he is putting constraint upon himself, doing all he can to make corrupt nature the servant of the spirit.

Much better to get rid of your sins now, prune away your bad habits here, than keep them to be paid for hereafter; it's only our preposterous attachment to creature comforts that blinds us.

3. Those fires, what is it they will feed on but your sins? The more you spare yourself, and take corrupt nature for your guide, the heavier price you will pay later on, the more fuel you are storing up for those fires. The pattern of a man's sins will be the pattern of his punishment; red-hot goads to spur on the idle, cruel hunger and thirst to torment the glutton; see where the dissipated souls, that so loved their own pleasures, are bathed in hot pitch and reeking sulphur, where the envious souls go howling like mad dogs, for very grief!

4. Each darling sin will find its appropriate reward; for the proud, every kind of humiliation, for the covetous, the pinch of grinding poverty. Spend a hundred years of penance here on earth, it would be no match for one hour of that punishment. Here we have intervals of rest, and our friends can comfort us; there is no respite for the damned, no consolation for the damned.

Take your sins seriously *now*, be sorry for them *now*, and at the Day of Judgement you will have confidence, the confidence of blessed souls. How fearlessly, then, the just will confront those persecutors of theirs, who kept them down all the time! The man who submitted to human judgements so meekly will now take rank as judge; in perfect calm they will stand there, the poor, the humble, while the proud are daunted by every prospect that meets them.

5. We shall see, then, what the true wisdom was—learning how to be a fool, and despised, for the love of Christ; troubles endured with patience will be a grateful memory to us, and it will be the turn of the wicked to look foolish. See how all pious souls make merry, and the scoffers go sad; how the body that was mortified shews fairer, now, than if it had been continually pampered; how rags are all the wear, and fine clothes look shabby; how the gilded palace shrinks into insignificance beside the poor man's cottage! The dogged patience you shewed here will do you more good than all earth's crowns; you will get more credit for unthinking obedience than for any worldly wisdom.

6. Philosophy will be less consolation to you than a good clean conscience, and all the treasures on earth won't outweigh the contempt of riches. The devout prayers you offered, not the good meals you ate, will be your comfort then. The silence you kept, not the long chats you had, will be pleasant to think of then. Saintly deeds done, not phrases neatly turned, will avail you then. A well-disciplined life of hard penitential exercise, not a good time here on earth, will be your choice then.

You have got to realize that all your sufferings here are slight ones,[20] and will get you off much worse sufferings hereafter. How much will you be able to stand there? The amount you can stand here is a good test. You, who find it so hard to bear these pin-pricks, how will you be able to take eternal punishment? What will you make of hell, when you make such a to-do about small discomforts?

No, you can't have your own way twice over; you can't take your pleasure in this world and then reign with Christ.

7. And now, suppose you had lived all your life, and were still living today, surrounded with honours and pleasures, what use would it all be, if you were to fall down dead this instant? Everything, you see, is just meaningless, except loving God and giving all our loyalty to him.

Love God with all your heart, and you've nothing to fear; death or punishment, judgement or hell; love, when it reaches its full growth, is an unfailing passport to God's presence. If we are still hankering after our sinful habits, of course we are afraid of death and judgement. Just as well, all the same, that if love can't succeed in beckoning us away from evil courses, we should be scared away by the fear of hell. Only, if a man doesn't make the fear of God[21] his first consideration, his good resolutions won't last; he will walk into some trap of the Devil's before long.

5. ON ACKNOWLEDGING OUR OWN WEAKNESS; AND ON THE MISERIES OF THIS LIPE

The Learner: Lord, I will tell you frankly, and to my shame, how sinful I am, how weak. It's often something quite trivial that upsets me and throws me out of balance. I make up my mind to take a firm line in the matter, and then, the moment the slightest temptation comes along, I find myself in a very tight corner. It's sometimes something quite petty that gives rise to a really serious temptation; I'm feeling fairly safe, and then, before I know what's happening, I sometimes find myself almost knocked over by the lightest gust.

2. So you see, Lord, how wretchedly frail I am; everything in the world will have told you that. Have pity on me; "save me from sinking in the mire"; don't let me stay down all the time. That is what often distresses me and shames me in your sight; that I am so apt to fall, so weak in resisting my passions. Even though I don't give way to them altogether, the way they keep on at me all the time is very irksome and distressing; I get sick and tired of living day in, day out, at war with myself. All this shews me how weak I am; the most loathsome fancies always rush in upon me much more readily than they take their leave.

3. Most powerful God of Israel, passionate lover of faithful souls, look upon the toil and trouble of this servant of yours; stand by him in all he sets his hand to. Strengthen me with heavenly courage; otherwise, the man I was once by nature, the wretched flesh not yet fully subject to the spirit, may be strong enough to overcome me. It is against this that I shall have to struggle so long as I draw breath in this sorry life. And oh, what a life it is! One long series of troubles and miseries, everything full of hidden traps and enemies! As soon as one trial or temptation takes itself off, along comes another; and while the first battle is still on, up come several more, out of the blue.

4. How can people love life, riddled as it is with bitterness, the prey of so many disasters and miseries? The very word "life" is surely a misnomer for something so prolific in death and misery. And yet it is loved, and there are many who seek all their pleasures from it. The world is often blamed for being deceitful and vain; yet it is not readily given up—fleshly desires have far too strong a say. There are some things that lead men to love the world, others that move them to despise it. The things that lead men to love the world are *gratification of corrupt nature, gratification of the eye, the empty pomp of living*,[22] but the penalties and miseries that rightly follow in the wake of these things fill men with disgust and hatred of the world.

5. But the sorry fact is that a distorted notion of pleasure conquers the mind that has surrendered to the world; it deems that enjoyment is to be found underlying the senses. The reason for this is that it has neither seen nor tasted the sweetness of God and the inward delight of holiness. But those who utterly despise the world and strive to live for God under a holy rule of life, are far from being unaware of that divine sweetness promised to all who really do renounce the world. They see more clearly than other men how sorely the world is astray, how manifold are its departures from the truth.

6. ABOUT HOLY SORROW

If you want to make any progress, the fear of God must be always about you: don't expect to be wholly free from restraint. You will have to keep all your senses under control, instead of giving yourself up to thoughtless enjoyment. Indulge, rather, your heart's sorrow; that way lies devotion. A sorrowing heart is the key to so many blessings which a wasted hour can easily fritter away! It's surprising, isn't it, that man's heart can ever be really contented in this life, when he reflects seriously on his exiled state, on the many dangers his soul runs?

2. Frivolity of mind, and carelessness about our faults, deaden us to the sense of our souls' misery; and so, as often as not, we find ourselves giving way to empty laughter, when there is good reason for tears. There can be no real freedom, no enjoyment worth having, unless the fear of God, and a good conscience, goes with it.

Well for you, if you can manage to clear all distractions out of the way, and concentrate on a single point—the exercise of holy sorrow. Well for you, if you can say good-bye to all that leaves a stain behind it, and burdens the conscience. Strive hard to reach that goal; habit must be formed, if habit is to be overcome. People will not let you go your own way? Yes, they will, if you leave them to go theirs.

3. Don't make other people's business your business; watch your own step all the time, and don't waste all your good advice on your friends; keep the best of it for yourself.

No need to be depressed, if you find that your fellow men don't think much of you; what ought to be weighing on your mind is that you are not behaving like a true servant of God, like a good religious—that is where you need to improve, to be more on the watch. Quite often we shall find it does us more good, and involves less risk, if we don't get much comfort out of this life, especially where human comfort is concerned. If we get little or no supernatural comfort either, that is our own fault; we haven't set our hearts on holy sorrow, and so we don't go the whole way in renouncing the paltry enjoyments of sense.

4. As for supernatural comfort, be sure you have done nothing to deserve it; affliction, and plenty of it, is all you deserve.

Once a man is master of this craft of sorrow, how full of weariness and bitterness the whole world seems to him! Look where he will, a good Christian man finds much to make him weep for sorrow; whether he looks into his own heart, or looks round at other people, he soon realizes that there's no such thing in this world as a life free from trouble. And the more carefully he looks into his own heart, the more deeply will he feel it; after all, what are the real grounds for our regret, for this inward sorrow? Our sins, those vicious habits of ours, that hardly ever let us think about heavenly things, so completely are we wrapped up in them.

5. If you thought more about death, and less about the years that lie ahead of you, you couldn't help being more eager to amend your life. And again, if you reflected seriously on the punishments that await you, whether in hell or in purgatory, I feel

certain you would be more ready to put up with difficulty and suffering; no hardship would have any terrors for you. But there it is—these things don't get in under the skin; we are still in love with the allurements of sense; that's why there's no fire in us, no energy.

6. Often, when our wretched bodies are quick to complain, the trouble is weakness of the spirit.

Pray to the Lord humbly, then, for this gift of sorrow; say, in the words of the sacred author, *Lord, allot me for food, for drink, only the full measure of my tears.*

7. A VIEW OF MAN'S MISERY

Wretched you needs must be, wherever you are and wherever you turn, unless you turn to God. Why make all this to-do about thwarted wishes, and blighted hopes? Was there ever man that got his own way all the time? Of course not, neither you nor I nor anybody else in the world—everybody has some troubles, some difficulties to put up with, kings and Popes like the rest of us. And who comes off best? The man who can stand up to a certain amount of suffering for the love of God.

2. Plenty of people can't—weak, flabby natures, that are always complaining, "Look at So-and-so; what a good time he has! How rich, how important he is; what influence and rank he enjoys!" But in reality, if you take one look at the prizes of heaven, you will see that all these earthly ones count for nothing; if anything, it is a weight on our minds, the precarious possession of them, a constant source of anxiety and alarm. Man's happiness doesn't consist in having more earthly possessions than he knows what to do with; a moderate fortune is all he needs.

A life of wretchedness, that's what our life on earth is. The higher a man's spiritual aims, the more distasteful does our present life appear to him; he sees more clearly, feels more deeply, the disabilities of our fallen nature. He must eat and drink, sleep and wake, labour and rest—all these natural needs have their claim on him, and it makes a devout soul feel wretched and harassed; why can't he be clear of it all, beyond the reach of sin? Do you doubt that bodily needs are a heavy burden to the spiritual man? Then why does the sacred author pray so earnestly to be delivered from them—*Lord, deliver me from my needs*?

But it will go hard with the people who don't realize their own wretchedness; harder still with those who are in love with this wretched, perishable life. There are people who so cling to it, even when they can scarcely support it by hard work, or on charity, that they would never give the kingdom of God a thought, if they had the chance of living here endlessly.

4. Minds without sense, hearts without faith! So deeply rooted in earth's soil, they have no appetite but for material things. Alas, when their end comes, these people will be wretched still! Then they will begin to realize how worthless and how unreal were the things they loved on earth. Whereas God's Saints, and all that were true friends of Christ, have always been indifferent to what gratified nature, to the hopes that bloomed so fair on earth; all their hope, all the set of their minds, aspired to the joys that are eternal. Upward it went, the whole longing of their hearts, to reach the abiding things, the things that are not seen; there should be no love of things seen, to drag them down to the depths.

No need, brother, to lose heart about your spiritual progress; time and opportunity are still yours.

5. Why postpone your good resolutions? Up with you, and set about it this instant; tell yourself, "Now is the time for action; this is zero-hour, just the right moment for making something better of my life". But you are feeling low, and finding things

difficult? Why, that is the very opportunity you want, to win your spurs! Of course you must pass through fire and water, before you can reach the cool shade. Put constraint on yourself, or never a fault will you overcome.

This body of ours is a weak instrument; so long as we carry it about with us, we have not said good-bye to sin, and we have not said good-bye to fatigue and unhappiness either. All very well, to wish we could be eased of our wretchedness, but there it is— by sinning, we have lost our innocence, and all true happiness with it. Patience, then, patience; we must wait for God's mercy to relieve us; wait till the curse is lifted, and our mortal nature is swallowed up in life.

6. What a feeble thing is this human nature of ours, always ready to slip down-hill! The sin you commit today is the same sin you mentioned yesterday in confession; an hour has gone by, and those resolutions about avoiding it might just as well not have been made. Haven't we good reason to feel ashamed? Can we ever entertain a good opinion of ourselves, weak and wavering creatures as we are? A moment's carelessness, and we have lost ground—the ground grace had won for us after such long, such painful struggles!

7. So early in the day, and already we are taking it easy! What state shall we be left in, at the day's end? Heaven help us, if we propose to turn in and take a rest, as if all were quiet and safe, when our life doesn't, even now, shew a single trace of genuine holiness! It would do us no harm at all if we could go back to the innocent days of our novitiate, and start training for perfection all over again; in that way, at least, we might hope to mend our ways for the future, and make more advance than we do at present in the ways of the spirit.

8. ON NOT BEING CONCERNED WITH OUTWARD THINGS

The Beloved: There are a good many things, my son, about which you should be ignorant. You ought to think of yourself as being dead, though still on earth; the whole world ought to seem to you as dead as if it were nailed to a cross. There are a lot of things it is as well to turn a deaf ear to; far better to think of things that keep your mind at peace. It is better to look the other way when you see something not to your liking, better to leave everyone to think as he pleases than to feel bound to begin a heated argument. If you are pleasing in the sight of God and are concerned only with his view of the matter in question, you won't mind it so much when you are worsted by others.

2. *The Learner*: Lord, what a state things have got into these days! You know how miserable we get over some worldly loss, and how we work hard and rush around to gain some little advantage; as for the damage done to our spiritual life, we quickly forget about it and even later on can scarcely call it to mind. We give all our attention to things that do us little good, or none at all; things that are vitally necessary we don't bother about and just give them the go-by. Yes, all that goes to make man drives him to meddle with outward things, and if he doesn't soon recover his senses, he is only too glad to wallow in material interests and pleasures.

9. ON THE ROYAL ROAD OF THE HOLY CROSS

"Renounce yourself, take up your cross and follow Jesus." There are many to whom that seems a hard saying; but how much harder will it be to hear that word of final judgement: *Go far from me, you that are accursed, into eternal fire.*[14] Those who now gladly hear the word of the cross and keep what it commands will not be afraid then when they hear the doom of everlasting loss. It is this sign of the cross that will appear in the sky when the Lord comes to judge us. Then all the servants of the cross, who during their lifetime made the Crucified the pattern of their deeds, will come with great confidence before Christ who is to judge them.

2. Why, then, are you afraid to take up your cross? It is your road to the kingdom of Christ. In the cross lies our salvation, our life; in the cross we have a defence against our foes. In the cross we have a pouring-in of heavenly sweetness, a strengthening of our minds and spiritual joy. In the cross is the peak of virtue, the perfection of holiness. There is no salvation for our souls, no hope of life everlasting, but in the cross. Take up your cross, then, and follow Jesus; and you will go into life that has no end. He has gone ahead of you, bearing his own cross; on that cross he has died for you, that you may bear your own cross and on that cross yearn to die. If you have died together with him, together with him you will have life; if you have shared his suffering you will also share his glory.

3. You see, the cross is at the root of everything; everything is based upon our dying there. There is no other road to life, to true inward peace, but the road of the cross, of dying daily to self. Walk where you will, seek whatever you have a mind to; you will find no higher road above, no safer road below, than the road of the holy cross. You may make all your plans and arrangements in accordance with your own notions and desires; even so, you will always find you have some suffering to bear, whether you like it or not; you will always find the cross.

Either you will be conscious of bodily pain, or your soul will be inwardly in distress.

4. Sometimes God will leave you to yourself, sometimes your neighbour will get on your nerves; what is worse, you will often become burdensome to your own self. No remedy or comfort will have power to free you from this condition, to make it easier to bear; you must put up with it as long as God so wills. God wants you to learn to bear suffering without anything to comfort you, to surrender yourself completely to him, to gain in humility by passing through distress. There is no one who so deeply realizes what Christ went through as the man who has had to suffer as he did. The cross, then, is at all times ready for you; never a place on earth but you will find it awaiting you. Dash off here or there, you can't get away from it; because, wherever you go, you take yourself along with you, and at every moment you will find yourself. Look above yourself or below, outside yourself or within; everywhere you will find the cross. And everywhere you must keep patient, if you would have inward peace and gain an everlasting crown.

5. If you carry your cross willingly, it will carry you and bring you to the goal for which you long. There, as you know, suffering will come to an end; but that won't be

while you are still here. If you grudge carrying your cross, it becomes a burden that weighs you down all the more; yet carry it you must. If you reject one cross, you will certainly find another; and this time it may not be so light.

6. Do you think you can escape something that never mortal man has been able to avoid? Think of the Saints; which of them spent his time in this world without the cross, without suffering? Why, even our Lord, Jesus Christ, was never for a single hour free from pain and suffering the whole of his lifetime. *Was it not to be expected*, he said, *that the Christ should undergo these sufferings, and enter so into his glory?*[15] Then how can you look for any other road than this royal road, the road of the holy cross?

7. The whole life of Christ was a cross and a martyrdom; and you go looking for rest and mirth! If you look for anything else but suffering to bear, you are right off the road; because the whole of this mortal life is full of misery, marked with crosses in every direction. The higher a man rises in the ways of the spirit, the weightier will he often find his crosses becoming. That is because the more his love of God grows, the more painful he feels this state of exile from him.

8. Such a man, however, afflicted as he is in so many ways, does not lack consolation to relieve him, because he realizes how great profit he is acquiring by bearing his cross. For while he willingly surrenders himself to it, his whole burden of suffering is changed into confident hope that God will console him. The more the flesh is weakened by suffering, the more is the spirit strengthened by means of inward grace. It not seldom happens that a man is so strengthened by his desire for suffering and adversity, the effect of his love that would follow the pattern of the cross of Christ, that he has no wish ever to be free from pain and suffering. This is because of his belief that the more affliction he has been able to bear for God's sake, the heavier to endure, the more pleasing he will be in God's sight. All this does not come from a man's own strength, but from the grace of Christ, which can have so powerful an effect, working as it does in our weak human nature; so that what a man of his nature shrinks from and seeks to escape he will go to meet and choose to love, through the fire of the spirit that burns within him.

9. Man by himself is not given to bearing crosses or loving them; to chastening his body and making it his slave; to avoiding honours and willingly brooking insults; to thinking little of himself and hoping that others will do the same. It is not his way to put up with all kinds of opposition and loss and not to desire any prosperity in this world. If you look only to yourself, all this kind of thing will be beyond your power; but if you put your trust in the Lord, you will be given strength from heaven, enabled to lord it over the world and the flesh. Even your enemy, the Devil, will be powerless to make you afraid, if you wear the armour of faith and are signed with the cross of Christ.

10. Set out, then, as a good and faithful servant of Christ, to bear like a man the cross of your Lord, that cross to which he was nailed for love of you. Be prepared to endure much thwarting and many a difficulty in this life of sadness; because that's how things are going to be for you, wherever you are, that's how you're sure to find things, wherever you look for shelter from them. That's the way it's got to be; there's

no cure, no getting round the fact of trouble and sorrow; you just have to put up with them. If you long to be the Lord's friend, to share what is his, you must drink his cup and like it. As for consolations, let God see about that; he will arrange about that kind of thing as he sees best. Your job must be to be ready to endure troubles and to reckon them the greatest of comforts; for what we suffer in this present life is nothing when we compare it with the glory to be won in the life to come, even though you alone were able to endure it all.

11. When you have reached such a point that trouble is sweet to you, something to be relished for Christ's sake, you may reckon that all is well with you; you have found heaven on earth. But so long as suffering irks you, so long as you try to avoid it, things will go ill with you; everywhere you will be pursued by the pain you try to escape.

12. If you resolve, as you ought, to suffer and to die, things will at once go better with you and you will find peace. Even if, like St. Paul, you were to be caught up to the third heaven, that would be no guarantee of your suffering no further affliction. *I have yet to tell him*, says Jesus, *how much suffering he will have to undergo for my name's sake.*[16] You have still to suffer, then, if you wish to love Jesus and serve him for ever.

13. If only you were worthy to suffer in some way for the name of Jesus! What great glory you would have awaiting you! How all the Saints of God would rejoice! And think how you would strengthen the spiritual life of your neighbour! All men agree in applauding patience in suffering; few are willing to suffer. You ought gladly to suffer a little for Christ's sake; there are many who suffer far worse for worldly interests.

14. Make no mistake about it; the life you are to lead must be one of death-in-life. The more a man dies to himself, the more he begins to live to God. No one is fit to grasp heavenly things unless he resigns himself to bearing affliction for Christ's sake. There is nothing more acceptable to God, nothing so conducive to your soul's health in this world, than willingly to suffer for Christ's sake. If you had the choice, you ought to choose rather to suffer affliction for Christ's sake than to be refreshed by much comfort; that would make you resemble Christ more nearly, make you follow more closely the pattern of all the Saints. Our merit, you see, our progress in virtue, doesn't consist of enjoying much heavenly sweetness and consolation; no, it lies in bearing heavy affliction and trouble.

15. If there had been anything better for men, more profitable for their salvation, than suffering, you may be sure that Christ, by his teaching and by his own example, would have pointed it out. But no; addressing the disciples who were following him, and all those who wish to follow him, he clearly urges them to carry the cross, when he says: *If any man has a mind to come my way, let him renounce self, and take up his cross, and follow me.*[17] So then, when we have made an end of reading and studying, this is the conclusion we should reach at last: *that we cannot enter the kingdom of heaven without many trials.*[18]

10. ON PURITY Of MIND, AND SINGLENESS OF PURPOSE

There are two wings that lift a man from the ground, singleness of heart and purity; the one regulates your intentions, the other your affections. The single-hearted man makes for God; the pure-minded man finds and enjoys him. No right course of action will have difficulties for you,[3] if only you're free in your own heart, free from ill-regulated desires. Such freedom will only come to you in full measure when you've made God's will and your neighbour's good your sole aim, your sole consideration.

If the dispositions of your heart were really true, everything in the world would be a mirror reflecting eternity, a book to teach you heavenly wisdom. After all, there's no creature in the world so mean and insignificant that it doesn't reflect, somehow, the glory of God.

2. You'd see everything with clear eyes, fit everything into the pattern of your thought, if goodness and purity were at the roots of your being. The pure heart has a range of vision that can reach the heights of heaven, the depths of hell. It's what he is in himself that determines a man's judgement of what lies outside himself. If there is such a thing as enjoyment in this world, it's an innocent mind that has the key to it; and if there is real misery and frustration to be found anywhere, go to the man with a bad conscience—he will tell you about it.

Put a bar of iron in the fire, and all the rust disappears; there's nothing but a uniform white glow. And so it is when a man turns right round towards God; the indifference flakes off him, and you've got a new man to deal with.

3. The moment you begin to lose interest, how formidable is the least effort! How gladly you distract your mind with worldly things! Whereas the moment you tackle the business of self-conquest thoroughly, and trudge manfully along the path of God's will, you make no account of the difficulties that seemed, till now, insurmountable.

11. TRUE COMPORT SHOULD BE SOUGHT IN GOD ALONE

The Learner: Whatever I can desire, whatever my thoughts can conceive in the way of comfort, I look to find not here, but later on. Even though I alone had all the comforts of the world, even though I could revel in all its pleasures, they could not last for long, that's certain. That is why my soul will never be able to find fullness of comfort, never be perfectly refreshed, save only in God, the comforter of the poor and refuge of the humble. Wait but a little while, my soul, wait for God to keep his promise, and in heaven you will have good things of all kinds, overflowing the cup of his bounty. But if you are full of uncontrolled yearning for the good things of this present life, you will lose those which belong to heaven and eternal life. Let the things of time be for you to use, but those of eternity the goal of your longings. None of the good things of this world can satisfy you; it was not to enjoy them alone that you were created.

2. Even though you possessed every good thing God has made, it could not make you happy and blessed; no, it is in God, who made all these things, that your whole blessedness lies, your whole happiness. I don't mean the kind of happiness envisaged by those foolish enough to love the world, the kind that earns their approval; no, I mean that happiness to which good and faithful followers of Christ look forward, that happiness of which a foretaste is sometimes given to the spiritual and the pure in heart, whose earthly lives are spent in heaven. All the comfort we get from human sources is empty and soon gone; true comfort, blessed comfort, is that which is inwardly given by the Truth. A devout man, wherever he may be, takes everywhere with him his comforter, Jesus, and says to him: "Be with me, Lord Jesus, at every moment and in every place." Let this, then, be my comfort, my willingness to forgo all comfort that comes from man; and if I do not receive your comfort, let my highest comfort be the thought that it is by your will, your justice, that I am thus being tested; because *he will not always be finding fault, his frown does not last for ever.*[20]

12. GOD, ABOVE ALL THINGS AND IN ALL THINGS, IS THE DELIGHT OF THE LOVING HEART

The Learner: My God, my all, you are here; what more can I wish for, what greater happiness can I desire?

O sweet and delightful word! But sweet only to those who love the Word, not to those who love the world and all that is in the world. My God, my all! To one who understands, that is enough said; to one who loves, it is something to be said over and over again, each time with joy. When you are present, there is joy in everything; when you are not, all things are distasteful. You set the heart at rest, you bring great peace and joy and mirth. You make us think well of all and praise you in all. There is nothing that can please us for long without you; but if it is to be enjoyable and to our taste, your grace must be within it, it needs to be flavoured with the spice of your wisdom.

2. When a man finds delight in you, what is there he will not find delight in? When a man takes no delight in you, what will be able to give him pleasure? But those who are wise in a worldly way, those who have the wisdom of the sensualist, are lacking in your wisdom; the former have nothing but utter emptiness, the latter find death. But those who by scorning worldly ways and chastening their bodily desires follow your own path, they are the really wise men; they have passed from empty folly to truth, from the flesh to the spirit. For such as these, God is their keenest delight: if they do find any good in creatures, they make it an additional reason for praising their Maker. But oh! how different, how immeasurably different, is the delight to be found in the Creator and that in things created; how little does eternity resemble time, or uncreated Light the borrowed brightness of creation!

3. O light unending, O light surpassing all that shines in your creation, send down from on high the lightning-stroke of your dazzling brilliance, to pierce and free from darkness the most secret depths of my heart! Seize my spirit and all its powers; give it your purity, your gladness, your brightness, your life, that it may cling to you in an ecstasy of joy. Ah, when will it come, that blissful and longed-for hour, when the joy of your presence shall brim to overflowing the depths of my desire, and you be my all in all? Until you grant me that, my joy cannot be full. Still does the man I was—I grieve to say it—stir to life within me; he is not completely nailed to the cross, not finally and utterly dead. Still do his lusts make violent war against the spirit, making my heart the battle-ground of civil war, so that the kingdom of my soul may not be at peace.

4. Arise and help me, my God, you who govern the might of the sea and calm the turbulent waves! Scatter the nations that delight in war; let that power of yours crush them. Shew them, I beg you, what mighty things you can do, and let them see the glorious power that lies in your hand; but for you, O Lord my God, I have no hope, no place where I may find shelter.

13. ON LOVING JESUS MORE THAN ANYTHING

It is a happy man that understands what is meant by loving Jesus and by despising oneself for his sake. You must renounce your other loves for the love of him, for Jesus desires to be loved alone more than all things else. When you love creatures, that love deceives you and never stays the same; when you love Jesus, your love is loyal and lasts. The man who clings to anything created will fall together with that fallible creature; if he holds fast to Jesus he will stay firm for ever. Give your love to him and keep him as your friend. When all others go away from you, he will not leave you or let you perish when the end comes. The day will come when, whether you like it or not, you must be parted from all men else.

2. In life and in death keep close to Jesus and give yourself into his faithful keeping; he alone can help you when all others fail you. He is of such a kind, this beloved friend of yours, that he will not share your love with another; he wishes to have your heart for himself alone, to reign there like a king seated on his rightful throne. If only you knew the way to empty your heart of all things created! If you did, how gladly would Jesus come and make his home with you! When you put your trust in men, excluding Jesus, you will find that it is nearly all a complete loss. Have no faith in a reed that shakes in the wind, don't try leaning upon it; *mortal things are but grass*, remember, *the glory of them is but grass in flower*[6] and will fall. Look only at a man's outward guise and you will quickly be led astray; look to others to console you and bring you benefit, and as often as not you will find you have suffered loss. If you look for Jesus in everything, you will certainly find him; but if it's yourself you're looking for, it's yourself you're going to find, and that to your own hurt, because a man is a greater bane to himself, if he doesn't look for Jesus, than the whole world is, or the whole host of his enemies.

14. EVERYTHING IS TO BE SEEN IN ITS RELATION TO GOD, OUR LAST END

The Beloved: If you really want to be happy, my son, you must make me your supreme and final end. Too frequently your affections stoop down to embrace yourself and things created; direct them on me, and they will be cleansed. When you seek yourself in anything, you at once lose heart and grow dry within. You ought therefore to refer everything chiefly to me; after all, it is I who have given you everything. Look upon each particular thing as flowing forth from the supreme good; that is the reason why it is to me, as to their origin, that all things must be brought back.

2. From me, as from a living spring, all men draw the water of life, little and great alike, rich and poor. Those who serve me freely and willingly shall receive grace for grace; but the man who would glory in anything apart from me, delight in some good of his own, will have no firm foothold in real joy. His heart will not be opened wide within him, but in a multitude of ways he will be thwarted and hemmed in. So, then, don't go writing good deeds down on your own account and don't attribute goodness to any man; give it all to God, without whom man has nothing. I have given you all, and I want to have it all back; what I ask of you, and that with great insistence, is that you should be thankful.

3. There you have the truth, the truth that sends vainglory about its business. If heavenly grace gains entrance to your heart, together with real charity, there will be no envy there, no shrivelling of the heart, no monopolizing of your affections by any particular love. The divine charity overcomes everything, gives every power of the soul room to expand. If you are really wise, you will place all your joy, all your hope, in no one but me, because *none is good except God only*,[14] and he is above all things to be praised, and in all things blessed.

15. ALL TROUBLES MUST BE BORNE FOR THE SAKE OF ETERNAL LIFE

The Beloved: My son, do not let the hard work you have taken on for my sake crush you; do not let any trouble make you lose heart completely. In all that happens, let my promise be your strength and consolation. The reward I have in store for you is both boundless and measureless. The time you are working here will not be long; you will not always have sorrows pressing upon you. Wait but a little while, and you will see all your miseries vanish in a trice. The time is coming when all your toil and trouble will be no more; anything that passes with the passing of time cannot but be short-lived, cannot but matter little.

2. Go on with what you are doing; work faithfully in my vineyard; the reward you will have is myself. Go on writing, reading, singing, sighing, keeping silence, bearing your troubles like a man; it is well worth fighting all your present battles, and even greater ones, to gain eternal life. Peace will come at a time known only to the Lord; there will not be day and night as we know them now, but light that never wanes, brightness that has no bounds, peace never to be broken, rest that shall never be disturbed. You will not say then, *Who is to set me free from a nature thus doomed to death?*[47] neither will you cry, *Unhappy I, that the days of my sojourn have been prolonged!*[48] for death will be cast headlong, and salvation no more be in danger; no anguish then to torment you, but only blessed joy, and the sweet and lovely companionship of heaven.

3. If only you had seen the crowns of unfailing glory worn by the Saints in heaven, seen how greatly they now rejoice there, though once the world scoffed at them and thought them hardly fit to live; you would certainly make yourself the lowest of the low and long to be at everyone's beck and call rather than lord it over a single person. You would not want to have a good time in this world, but be glad to endure trouble for God's sake; as for being thought nothing of by men, that would seem to you the greatest of advantages.

4. If you were really keen to get to heaven, if the thought of it went right home to your inmost heart, how would you have the affrontery to voice a single grievance? Surely, with eternal life as the prize, you ought to put up with all kinds of hardship. It's not a small matter, you know, this losing or gaining the kingdom of God. So look up to heaven; that is where I am, and with me all my Saints who in this life had a hard struggle of it; here at this very moment they are rejoicing, at this very moment comforted, safe and at rest; and here in the kingdom of my Father they will stay in my company for time without end.

16. ALL OUR HOPE AND TRUST MUST BE PLACED IN GOD ALONE

The Learner: Lord, what can I rely on in this life? What is my greatest comfort of all that can be seen under heaven? Is it not you, my Lord and my God, you whose mercy is beyond reckoning? Where have things gone well with me, with you not there? And when could things have gone badly for me, with you at my side? I had rather be poor for your sake than rich without you. I would choose to roam the world with you beside me than possess heaven and not you; but heaven is where you are, and where you are not—that is what death is, and hell. It is for you that I long; it is this longing that constrains me to sigh for you, to call out to you, to beg you for help. Finally, there is no one I can trust unreservedly, no one who in my need will help me at just the right moment, but you alone, my God. You are my hope, my trust, my comfort, always standing by me whatever happens.

2. All men seek their own advantage; all *your* scheming, Lord, is for my salvation, my betterment. Under your hands, everything turns out to be for my good. You may let me in for all sorts of trials and troubles, but you arrange for things to happen in that way only for my own good. Testing them in all sorts of fashions is a way you have of dealing with those whom you love; so when you test me like that I ought to love you and praise you just as much as if you were filling me with your heavenly consolation.

3. It is in you, then, Lord God, that I put all my hope, to you that I run for protection; in your hands I put all my troubles and misery. If I look at anything apart from you for help, I find nothing but uncertainty and doubtful stability. Having a lot of friends won't help me, having influential people to back me won't further my cause. If I ask the wise for advice, they can give me no answer I can act on; there can be no comfort for me in the books of the learned. No precious substance can buy my freedom, no private paradise afford me shelter. No, Lord, none of these can help me unless you yourself stand by me, helping me, strengthening and comforting me, instructing and keeping watch over me.

4. When you are not with me, everything that seems likely to bring me peace and happiness means nothing to me; things like that don't really make me happy. You are the goal for which all good men are striving; you are the highest peak of all that has life, the lowest deep that underlies all speech. Nothing is so great a comfort to your servants as to trust in you above all else. It is to you, my God, I raise my eyes, in you, O Father of mercies, that I place my trust. Bless and make holy this soul of mine with your heavenly blessing; so let it become a place sacred enough for you to dwell in it, a place where your eternal glory may stay for ever. Let nothing be found in this temple of your greatness on which your royal glance might light with disfavour. In the immensity of your goodness, the unmeasured stores of your mercy, look upon me and listen to the prayer of this poor servant of yours, so far from home here in the land of the shadow of death. Guard and keep the soul of this least of your servants amid the many dangers of this uncertain life. Give me your grace for my companion, and guide me along the path of peace, until I reach my true country, the land of unending light. Amen.

Enjoyed your Christian reading?

Don't end your introduction to Christian literature here.

Send a blank email to

thegoodchristian10@gmail.com

for access to Christian audiobooks.